Radical Sports
MOTOCROSS

Gary Freeman ● ● ● ● ● ● ● ● ● ●

Heinemann

D0337002

C152390979

H www.heinemann/library.co.uk

Visit our website to find out more information about Heinemann Library books.

To order:

☎ Phone 44 (0) 1865 888066

📄 Send a fax to 44 (0) 1865 314091

💻 Visit the Heinemann Library Bookshop at www.heinemann/library.co.uk to browse our catalogue and order online.

First published in Great Britain by Heinemann Library,
Halley Court, Jordan Hill, Oxford OX2 8EJ,
a division of Reed Educational and Professional Publishing Ltd.
Heinemann is a registered trademark of Reed Educational & Professional Publishing Limited.

OXFORD   MELBOURNE   AUCKLAND
JOHANNESBURG   BLANTYRE   GABORONE
IBADAN   PORTSMOUTH NH (USA)   CHICAGO

© Reed Educational and Professional Publishing Ltd 2002
First published in paperback 2003
The moral right of the proprietor has been asserted.

All rights reserved. No part of this publication may be reproduced, stored in a retrieval system, or transmitted in any form or by any means, electronic, mechanical, photocopying, recording, or otherwise without either the prior written permission of the Publishers or a licence permitting restricted copying in the United Kingdom issued by the Copyright Licensing Agency Ltd, 90 Tottenham Court Road, London W1P 0LP.

Designed by Celia Floyd
Illustration by Barry Atkinson
Originated by Universal
Printed in Hong Kong by Wing King Tong

ISBN 0 431 03691 8 (hardback)   ISBN 0 431 03699 3 (paperback)
06 05 04 03 02   07 06 05 04 03
10 9 8 7 6 5 4 3 2 1   10 9 8 7 6 5 4 3 2 1

British Library Cataloguing in Publication Data

Freeman, Gary
  Motocross. – (Radical sports)
  1. Motocross Juvenile literature
  1. Title
  796.7'56

KENT
ARTS & LIBRARIES
C152390979

Acknowledgements

The Publishers would like to thank the following for permission to reproduce photographs:
All photos by Gary Freeman except p5 Corbis and p13 Science Photo Library.

Cover photograph reproduced with permission of Gary Freeman.

Our thanks to Jane Bingham and Danny Walters for their help in the preparation of this book.

Every effort has been made to contact copyright holders of any material reproduced in this book. Any omissions will be rectified in subsequent printings if notice is given to the Publisher.

This book aims to cover all the essential techniques of this radical sport but it is important when learning a new sport to get expert tuition and to follow any manufacturers' instructions.

CONTENTS

What is Motocross?

Motocross is a type of motorcycle racing held on a rough and bumpy dirt track. The bikes used to race Motocross have fast, high-revving engines, chunky, knobbly tyres, and strong **suspension** to tackle the jumps and bumps.

To race in Motocross you need to be fit and strong because holding onto the bike is very tiring. Once you've mastered the basic techniques, Motocross quickly becomes one of the most exciting and enjoyable two-wheeled sports.

250cc World Championship riders hit the first turn of a race.

A brief history

The first ever Motocross races were held in the 1920s in the UK. In those days, Motocross was called 'scrambling' because the bikes quite literally scrambled their way around the rough and basic tracks. Before races were properly organized, riders used to go scrambling on any rough land they could find. Purpose-built Motocross bikes didn't exist, so normal road bikes were used – and the bumps and jumps soon took their toll.

The first Motocross bikes featured stronger suspension, number plates instead of lights, and tyres that would grip the dirt better. Although the bikes had developed a little, the kit had not – riders still wore rugby shirts, leather riding pants and goggles with thick glass.

Early motocross bikes were much more basic than the high-tech bikes of today, and the riding gear was heavy and uncomfortable.

Like many sports, Motocross can be dangerous if the proper safety equipment is not worn but, with care and a sensible approach to riding, Motocross can be fantastic fun.

Motocross has a huge following around the world. Most countries have youth and adult national championships. There are also European Championships, and the ultimate is the World Championships – only for adult racers, but still great to watch!

MOTOCROSS BIKES

Modern Motocross bikes are designed to take the hard knocks of off-road racing – they need good **suspension** to smooth out the terrain, fast-accelerating engines to zip out of tight corners, and powerful brakes that stop the bike in an instant. There are also some variations in off-road motorcycling like Enduro and Trials riding, as well as Freestyle.

Enduro

Enduro riders race against the clock and try to ride around a very long course as fast as they can. Enduro tracks are usually laid out in woodland areas and feature obstacles such as tree trunks and roots, rivers or streams and even some road sections. The name Enduro is based on the fact that the winner is the rider who can endure the conditions the best.

Motocrossers love to race against each other – sometimes they fly too!

Very similar in design to a Motocross bike, Enduro bikes have smoother power and also feature lights for the road.

Trials

Trials riding is all about balance and control on the bike. Riders compete against each other indirectly by getting through a trials section in the fastest time, but can receive penalty points if their feet touch the ground or, of course, if they fall. Obstacles are either natural, such as a tree trunk, or man-made, such as a huge tyre from an earthmover.

A Trials bike engine is intended to be very powerful at slow speeds, which helps the rider up, over and through the obstacles found within a section of track. This means the suspension doesn't need to be as strong – and since the rider is always standing up there is no seat.

Freestyle

Just like inline skating, skateboarding and surfing, Motocross has its own Freestyle competitions. Many Freestyle riders may never have raced Motocross in competition, but just enjoy riding a Motocross bike at their local track for fun. Freestyle riders perform tricks and stunts on the bike and judges award them points.

Freestyle bikes are modified Motocross bikes. Most Freestyle riders will trim back the bike's plastic mudguards to help them to move around on the bike whilst in the air. They may also add grab handles to the rear of the bike or alternatively cut grab holes into the bike's plastics to help perform tricks.

Tricks are performed in mid-air during freestyle competitions.

CHOOSING THE RIGHT BIKE

Before you decide to buy a Motocross bike, the best thing to do is have a go on a smaller and less powerful Dirt bike. Motocross bikes are built for racing, so they're usually too fast for beginners. You can rent bikes at some local practice tracks. Many bike manufacturers also run 'try out' days where you can see if off-road motorcycle riding is for you.

Many beginners' bikes feature **four-stroke** engines rather than the **two-stroke** engines more commonly found in Motocross racers. The four-stroke engine is perfect for learning because it is more controllable.

Make sure that the first bike you try is small enough to allow you to comfortably touch the floor with both feet and that the engine is not too powerful. 80cc to 100cc engines usually have ample power for the beginner. It's always best to buy your first bike from a specialist Motocross dealer – that way you'll get lots of good advice too.

Rear shock absorber

Device which helps to smooth out movement from the swinging arm.

Brake disc

The metal disc is squeezed by the brake pads to stop the bike quickly.

TOP TIP

⚙ A second-hand bike can be a good bargain but you should always make sure that an expert has given it a thorough check before you decide to buy.

Chain

The chain is a string of metal links that runs around the bike's **sprockets**.

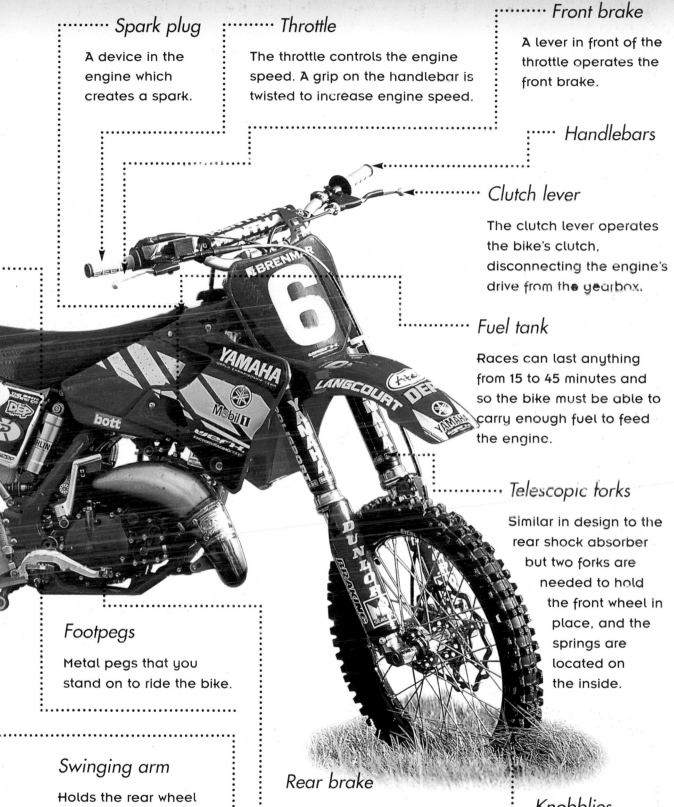

Spark plug

A device in the engine which creates a spark.

Throttle

The throttle controls the engine speed. A grip on the handlebar is twisted to increase engine speed.

Front brake

A lever in front of the throttle operates the front brake.

Handlebars

Clutch lever

The clutch lever operates the bike's clutch, disconnecting the engine's drive from the gearbox.

Fuel tank

Races can last anything from 15 to 45 minutes and so the bike must be able to carry enough fuel to feed the engine.

Telescopic forks

Similar in design to the rear shock absorber but two forks are needed to hold the front wheel in place, and the springs are located on the inside.

Footpegs

Metal pegs that you stand on to ride the bike.

Swinging arm

Holds the rear wheel in place and transfers the impact from bumps and jumps to the rear shock absorber.

Rear brake

A pedal in front of the right footpeg operates the rear brake.

Knobblies

Knobbly Motocross tyres.

THE RIGHT GEAR

Just like trying out a bike before you ride, it's also important to get used to wearing the right type of protective equipment. Some tracks have equipment to hire, but some bike manufacturers have 'try out' days, which are the best way to get a complete package – they may even give you a free lunch!

Motocross can be a dangerous sport if the right equipment is not worn. All equipment is available from specialised Motocross dealers. They may even have some second-hand kit – but never buy a second-hand helmet – you never know how much use it's had!

Body armour

Worn underneath your race shirt, plastic body armour protects you from flying stones and also protects your upper body if you crash.

Kneepads

Kneepads are essential and are worn under the race pants and usually held in place by Velcro fasteners.

SAFETY FIRST

⚙ Falling off a Motocross bike, even at slow speed, can be very painful if the right gear isn't worn. Always make sure you wear the right protective equipment when riding a Motocross bike. This way you'll enjoy the riding without taking unnecessary risks.

Helmet

Make sure it fits properly and carries the minimum safety standard markings.

Goggles

Lightweight plastic goggles must be worn at all times. Motocross goggles are very similar to ski goggles.

Shirt

Race shirts are usually made from cotton or polyester – there are also some aertex versions available.

Gloves

Motocross gloves are thin and made from synthetic suede. They do carry some knuckle protection, although if flying stones are a problem, hand guards attached to the handlebars should be used.

Pants

Race pants feature reinforced protective material with elasticised panels for good flexibility.

Boots

Made from tough leather, a smooth rubber sole and lots of shin protection, Motocross boots are an essential part of your kit.

KEEPING FIT AND HEALTHY

Keeping fit and healthy is vital if you are to take part in Motocross races. Exercises such as running, swimming and cycling are perfect for Motocross because they help your stamina and endurance.

When you train, make sure you're not rushing to finish the session. You'll get much more benefit from a long slow cycle, run or swim, than a fast sprint.

Practising and keeping fit on a mountain bike is great fun and is a perfect way to get used to riding on rough ground.

Eating well

To ride a Motocross bike you'll need to keep your body topped up with the right nutrients that give you energy. Also try to avoid eating a heavy meal before you ride. It is best to eat something light, such as cereals, bread or toast and fruit.

While you're out riding you should eat little and often. Fruit or energy bars are perfect to snack on, and you should also make sure you drink lots of water.

Brown bread, fruit and vegetables are excellent foods to eat to stay healthy.

Good foods to eat include pasta, baked potatoes and rice which are all great sources of carbohydrates. Fruit and vegetables are packed with vitamins and fibre and are also low in fat and calories. Both white meat and fish are good low fat sources of protein. Finally beans are rich in protein, dietary fibre and carbohydrates.

Foods to avoid are the ones high in saturated fats. Anything deep-fried in animal fats or vegetable oils should be avoided because they are high in fat, but low in other nutrients. Sweet food such as chocolate is also high in fat and not helpful for the body's performance.

Hydration

Keeping the body well hydrated is essential to maintain a good performance. If the body becomes dehydrated by even 2 per cent, then your performance will begin to suffer. Avoid sweet carbonated drinks. Sip water or fresh fruit juices throughout the day.

GETTING STARTED

The best place to learn to ride Motocross safely is at a 'try out' day.

Motocross training schools are an excellent way to quickly improve with the supervision and expertise of experienced tutors. They can quickly spot where you're going wrong and help you put it right.

Local races

Nowadays local races are held on most weekends by regional clubs. In most countries the racing season usually starts in March and runs through until October. You may also find some indoor racing – called 'Supercross' which is featured later in the book. It's really easy to join a club, and they all have regular club meetings away from the track.

Local races are a great place to watch and learn. Never be afraid to ask, everyone has to start somewhere and you'll find that Motocross riders will be pleased to help.

You can make great friends at a training school.

To find out where the nearest racing takes place ask at a local motorcycle or Motocross shop. The people in the shop are likely to race themselves and will be able to advise you on where to contact the nearest club.

A typical track

All Motocross tracks feature a start gate where the riders line up at the start of the race, but some Motocross practice tracks don't need a start gate because the track is used purely for practising, not racing.

Out on the track you'll definitely find lots of bumps, which range in size and shape. Some bumps are formed by the natural shape of the land, while some develop from the bikes bouncing over the dirt. Man-made bumps called **kickers** and **whoops**, made with earthmovers, also feature on some tracks. Most tracks also feature some jumps, which vary in size and shape and may include **tabletops**, **step ups** and ramp jumps.

This aerial view shows a race in progress.

BASIC TECHNIQUES

The best way to get to know the bike is to put it on a **box stand**. You should sit on it with your feet on the **footpegs** and hands gripping the handlebars.

On the right side of the handlebars you'll find the **throttle**, which controls the speed of the engine. In front of the throttle is the front brake lever which, when squeezed, slows down the front wheel. The rear brake is controlled by a foot pedal, which is found in front of the right footpeg. In front of the left footpeg is the gear lever. Most Motocross bikes have five or six gears.

On the left side of the handlebars, in front of the handgrip, is the clutch. Once the bike's engine is running and you're ready to set off, the clutch should be let out slowly with the bike in first gear. Letting the clutch out slowly gently introduces drive to the rear wheel – at the same time the throttle should be opened gradually to increase power to the engine. When you come to a stop, pull in the clutch and put the bike into neutral gear.

Standing position

Stand on the bike's footpegs, bend your back from the waist and bring your chest towards the **bar pad**. Your weight should be over the mid to rear of the bike. Shoulders should be positioned just behind the handlebars and your elbows should be kept high.

The standing position gives you good overall balance on the bike.

This position is perfect for general riding along straights and over bumps because it gives you a good overall balance on the bike.

Braking

When braking, you should try to put as much weight over the rear wheel as possible to help it grip. As you brake, you should also change down a gear or two depending on how slow your speed is. Brake with the front brake lever and rear brake pedal at the same time.

Racing starts

The start gate is a metal frame that drops towards the bikes at the start of a race. If you touch the gate before the starter releases your gate, it will not drop. To get a good start, your weight should be forward on the bike. Your head should look down to the start gate and your elbows should point up. When the gate drops, release the clutch and off you go.

Race starts are always a thrill, both to watch and to take part in.

Corners

To corner well, get your approach speed correct. Too slow, and the bike will feel unstable. Too fast, and you may run wide or overshoot the corner and go off the track. Use the **ruts** or **berms** in the corner for extra stability and introduce the power smoothly.

Watching professional riders blast out of a corner is really spectacular.

Regular jumps

Make sure that your weight is to the rear of the bike during take off. Once the bike is airborne, you can adjust its level by moving your weight forwards or backwards. When landing from a regular jump (including ramp jumps), you usually land on your rear wheel.

Tabletop jumps

A **tabletop** jump is a flat-topped jump with an **upslope** and **downslope** at the front and rear. The most effective way to land from a tabletop jump is to land on the front wheel first. As you take off, your weight should be to the rear of the bike. When in the air, move your weight forward to allow the front of the bike to drop forwards. You should land on the downslope of the tabletop with the front wheel first and then power away. Tabletops are usually quite big jumps, which produce lots of **airtime** and are great fun once you've mastered the technique.

Drop offs

Drop offs are sheer drops in the track, which you jump off to land on the track below. Most drop offs are very steep and so are difficult to ride down. The best way to tackle a drop off is to push your weight to the rear of the bike and keep the **throttle** open on take off. This helps to keep the front wheel higher up and allows the rear wheel to touch the ground first. You should avoid front wheel landings from drop offs, as they can be dangerous.

When landing from regular jumps and drop offs it is important to land with the rear wheel first.

TOP TIP

⚙ The standing position for general riding is the most efficient way to ride. This riding position will give you a good overall balance on the bike and help you in most situations to choose the best **racing line**.

TAKING IT FURTHER

To ride with the world's best in Motocross, you'll need to train extremely hard, both on the bike and off the bike for general fitness. Many Motocross riders are so fit they can quite easily compete in triathlon events, cycle races or running events.

The best way to improve is to get some one-to-one tuition. To find tutors check out Motocross magazines, or contact your home country's Motocross racing organization for information.

At the race

Riders always race against others of a similar age and bike size. Competitors are separated into classes and given a number, which must be displayed on the bike. The race schedule will usually be printed in the event programme and it may also be announced on a speaker system prior to the start.

Before the racing begins, riders are generally allowed a few laps of practice. Like the racing classes, riders will practise according to their age and bike size. Each class's practice session will last for around ten to fifteen minutes. Youth events usually feature three races per class, and races last for approximately fifteen minutes.

An ex-world champion offers help to a young hopeful.

Qualifying for a higher level

Riders usually earn points throughout the race season, and those with enough points are eligible to take part in National Championship qualifying races, which are held at designated local meetings throughout the country. This may mean you have to travel further afield to race in a National Championship qualifier – or you may be lucky and find your local club hosting a qualifying race themselves.

If you succeed in doing well in the qualifying races, then you can race in the National Championship races the following year. Most countries also hold national junior championships. Information on where and when these are held can be obtained by contacting your country's motorcycle sport governing body. The system of qualifying does vary from country to country so it's always best to check first.

These races are similar to local races, but the standard of riding will of course be higher so, if you make it, you'll need to be fit and have practised a lot.

The ultimate Motocross racing is at the Grand Prix where some of the world's best riders compete head to head and huge crowds go to watch.

RULES AND SAFETY

Motocross rules should never be broken. When they are, this fun sport can become dangerous.

At Motocross race meetings, race officials and track marshals should be present so make sure you familiarize yourself with all of the safety rules and flag signals. When you're racing, observe and obey the flag signals. They are there for everyone's safety.

Practising with friends is great fun, but whether practising or racing, protective clothing should always be worn.

SAFETY FIRST

- ☼ Never ride alone – if you fall and hurt yourself you may need help from a friend.

- ☼ When joining a track, never cross in front of an oncoming rider – it's very difficult to judge the speed of approaching bikes.

- ☼ Always wear your protective equipment – you'd be amazed how much even the smallest fall can hurt without your protective gear.

- ☼ Never allow petrol near a naked flame or lighted cigarette.

- ☼ If your bike breaks down in the middle of the track make sure you move it as quickly as possible to a safe place away from other bikes and riders.

- ☼ Never attempt something outside of your limits – improvement will come slowly without you realizing it. Never push yourself too far.

- ☼ Don't show off to spectators – Motocross is spectacular to watch but if you show off, chances are you'll not be concentrating on what you're doing. This can lead to embarrassing – and painful – falls.

Flag signals

At organized race meetings there should be a flag system in operation, used by track marshals who will be situated at designated points around the circuit. Before you race, you must familiarize yourself with the flags in use and know what to do, and what not to do, if you see one waved. Some flags are very common, but flags will vary between countries and organizations. It is vital that you check before you start.

Yellow flag: There is an obstruction (usually a fallen rider) in front of the yellow flag. Overtaking is strictly forbidden.

Red flag: The race is stopped. Stop your bike immediately, switch off the engine and await further instructions.

Blue flag: Be prepared to be passed or lapped by a leading rider or riders. Move away from the **racing line** to allow them through.

Black flag: You must leave the course at the designated track exit.

Chequered flag: The finisher's flag, signalling the end of the race.

White flag with red cross: First aid is needed for a fallen rider.

Maintaining a Motocross bike is essential for reliability. Your local Motocross dealer should be able to offer you a maintenance check and service of your bike. Local Motocross clubs also have members who can offer help and advice. Always get the help of an experienced adult.

Adjusting the chain

A slack chain can fly off and, if this happens when approaching a jump, it can be dangerous. Make sure the chain is tightened according to the bike's user manual. Never over-tighten the chain because this will put unnecessary pressure on the links and could cause it to stretch or snap.

Cleaning the air filter

A clean **air filter** is vital to ensure a good flow of air to the engine. As a rule, your air filter should be cleaned and oiled each time you ride your bike, but if it is clean after you've ridden, then don't clean it just for the sake of it. Many manufacturers sell air filter cleaning kits, which include plastic gloves, cleaning fluid, air filter oil and sealing grease.

To check if your bike's wheel spokes are tight, tap each one with the spoke wrench and listen for a pinging sound. All spokes should make more or less the same note as you strike them. If one makes a low note or thud, then it probably needs tightening. Spokes are tightened using the tightening screw just by the wheel rim.

Note: Sometimes the spokes will touch each other as they cross, and this can make them sound loose. Push one away from the other with your thumb as you check their tightness.

Replacing the spark plug

A new **spark plug** should last a long time, but it is good practice to replace them after four races, because the electrodes can become worn.

Changing the oil

Oil should be changed as often as possible, preferably after each race meeting. Make sure the engine is warm but not hot before the oil is drained – that way it's thinner and runs more easily. Undo the oil filler cap, and then undo the drain plug underneath the oil sump. Catch the old oil in a bucket or tray. Then replace the drain plug and refill the correct amount of oil as per the bike's maintenance handbook.

SAFETY FIRST

⚙ Make sure an expert shows you how to carry out the important maintenance checks on your bike, the first few times you do them.

⚙ Never fill up the petrol tank alone. Always ask for help from an adult.

What is Supercross?

Motocross is run on outdoor tracks and includes many natural features. But Supercross tracks are all made by huge earthmovers to shape and mould the dirt into a tight twisting labyrinth of bumps and jumps.

Supercross is most popular in the US. Race organizers build tracks in sports stadiums, which feature spectacular **tabletop** jumps, **killer whoop** sections and banked corners. The stadium atmosphere at a Supercross race is electrifying, with up to 100,000 crazed fans all with a bird's eye view of the racing below. The 16-race US National Supercross series runs from early January to early May each year. You'll also find that many European countries run a national Supercross series in the winter too.

What is Freestyle?

Freestyle riding mostly involves performing acrobatic tricks together with the bike in mid-air. Huge ramp jumps are made from wood and metal or dirt to allow the bike to be thrown high into the air. This allows the rider enough time to perform a trick or stunt, before landing safely.

Supercross is a spectacular variation of Motocross.

It takes many months of practice to perfect even the simplest of Freestyle tricks, and it can be extremely dangerous without skill, knowledge and supervision. The safest way to enjoy Freestyle is to watch!

Now Freestyle 'jump offs' are run as competition extravaganzas – and none are bigger than the annual Gravity Games held in the US. Freestyle jump offs are also held at Supercross and some Motocross events, between races. Check out the magazines and Internet for details.

The lazy boy freestyle trick.

FREESTYLE TRICKS

Here are some tricks to look out for:

- *Cliffhanger* The only thing that keeps the riders in touch with the bikes are their feet tucked behind the handlebars. This trick is really spectacular.

- *Candy Bar* In the air, the rider puts one leg over the handlebars, and then brings it back for landing.

- *Bar Hop* Both legs go over the handlebars in a crouched position. Wild!

- *Lazy Boy* Lay back across the whole bike in the air. Wake up before landing!

- *Can Can* While holding onto the bars, both legs are stuck out of the side, then returned for landing.

CHAMPIONSHIPS AND MOTOCROSS STARS

The best Motocross racing can be found at the FIM (Federation Internationale de Motorcyclisme) World Championships, which are held from mid-March to late September each year. There are approximately 16 World Championship races held at tracks throughout Europe each year and, on occasion, races are held in countries such as Australia, South America and the US.

The 12-round US National Motocross Championships also features racing at least equal to the standards found in the World Championships. Races are held from mid-May until early September throughout the US.

Most countries also run their own national championship, and many riders at these events also race in the World Championships.

Jamie Dobb

British rider Jamie Dobb began racing at the age of five and turned professional at fifteen. He went on to win four British Championships and is the 2001 125cc Motocross World Champion. During his career, Jamie also raced in the US and posted some fantastic results in the US National Championships.

British rider Jamie Dobb.

Stefan Everts

Belgian rider Stefan Everts is already a five-time World Motocross Champion, winning one title in the 125cc class in 1991, and three 250cc World Championships in 1995, 1996 and 1997. In 2001, Stefan switched to the 500cc class and went on to win his first World Championship on the big bikes.

Jeremy McGrath

Born in San Francisco, Jeremy McGrath is an ex-BMX racer turned Motocross professional. He started racing Motocross at the age of fourteen and registered his presence on the scene just four years later, posting eighth in the 125cc US Supercross series. He was second in 1990, and won in 1991 and 1992. Jeremy switched to the 250cc class in 1993 and won in the same year, then went on to win in 1994, 1995, 1996, 1998, 1999 and 2000.

Gordon Crockard

Gordon Crockard is from Newtownards in Northern Ireland. His first race was in 1990 at the age of twelve and, in 1992, he won the Irish Schoolboy Championship riding a 100cc Kawasaki. In 2000, Gordon won his first British Championship and followed that up with another win in 2001. Gordon also finished third in the 2001 World Championships.

Gordon Crockard from Northern Ireland.

GLOSSARY

air filter foam filter that prevents dirt and dust from being sucked into the engine

airtime the time you and the bike stay in the air when jumping

bar pad foam pad that covers the cross bar of the handlebars

berm small banking of dirt in a corner, used to lean the bike into

box stand box shaped main bike stand used to support the whole bike

downslope down-sloping landing ramp of a tabletop

drop off sheer drop that you jump off, then land on the track below

footpegs serrated metal bars which you put your feet on

four-stroke a type of motor that works like a car engine

kicker large bump in the track that kicks the bike up in the air

killer whoops man-made set of big bumps

racing line or **race line** also known as 'Line,' the fastest, and usually smoothest route around the track

rut grooves in the track that form when the dirt is moist or wet; ruts can also form in corners where bikes' rear tyres dig into the dirt

spark plug a device in the engine which creates a spark

sprocket a round plate with teeth to fit into the chain links

step up section of a jump that allows you to jump up and over the next (higher) jump

suspension springs and shock absorbers which help the bike to smooth out the bumps and jumps

tabletop flat-topped jump with an upslope and downslope at the front and rear

throttle twist grip that controls the engine speed

two-stroke a type of engine that uses petrol and oil to produce power

upslope up-facing ramp of a tabletop or step up jump

whoops man-made set of bumps

USEFUL ADDRESSES

Auto-Cycle Union UK
ACU House – Wood Street
Rugby
Warwickshire CV21 2YX
Website: www.motorcyclinggb.com
Tel: 01788 566400

Amateur Motor Cycle Association Ltd (AMCA)
28 Mill Park
Hawks Green Lane
Cannock
Staffs WS11 2XT
Website: www.amca.uk.com
Tel: 01543 466282

Motor Cycle Union of Ireland
BEAT Centre
Stephenstown Business Park
Balbriggan
Dublin
Email: mcuireland@yahoo.com
Website: www.mcui.ie
Tel: +353 1 802 0480

Australia

Motorcycling Australia
147–149 Montague Street
South Melbourne
Victoria 3205
Email: mail@motorcycling-aus.com.au
Tel: +61 3 9696 0955

World

Federation de Internationale Motorcyclisme
(FIM)
11, route Suisse
CH-1295 Mies
Switzerland
Email: info@fim.ch
Website: www.fim.ch/en

FURTHER READING

Books

To the limit: Motocross, Gary Freeman,
Hodder Children's Books, 2000

All the Internet addresses (URLs) given in this book were valid at the time of going to press. However, due to the dynamic nature of the Internet, some addresses may have changed, or sites may have ceased to exist since publication. While the author and publishers regret any inconvenience this may cause readers, no responsibility for any such changes can be accepted by either the author or the publishers.

Websites

www.motograndprix.com
The main site of the Motocross Grand Prix organizers. The best for detailed race results.

www.mx2k.com/us
Full of useful information in both French and English.

www.mxlarge.com
For the very latest news and results, there's nowhere better. The number one site in Europe.

INDEX